Golden
NUGGETS

GOLDEN NUGGETS
Devotionals

CECELIA CUTCHIN

Published
by Daughters of Distinction LLC

"Golden Nuggets"
Published by Daughters of Distinction LLC
Baltimore, MD USA

Copyright © 2020 by CECELIA CUTCHIN
All rights reserved. No part of the book may be
reproduced in any form without permission in writing
from the publisher, except in the case of brief quotations
embodied in articles or reviews

Printed in the United States of America

ISBN: 978-0-578-69823-6

Cover Design and Layout: Ebony Richardson

DEDICATION

I dedicate this book to my Mother, Minnie G. Gardner. She was a God-fearing woman that had a giving heart. She lived, as I do, by the scripture Luke 6:31" Do to others as you would have them do to you."

I also dedicate this book to my close friend who was like a sister. Patty J. Hopkins was my friend, confidant, and mentor. She was a true Prophet of God and is missed every day. I thank God for blessing my life with these two amazing women.

Table of Contents

CHAPTER 1   page#
Winter

- Wine — 17
- Change — 18
- Fit — 20
- Credit — 21
- Lean — 22
- Wash — 23
- Look — 24
- Tools — 26
- Need — 27
- Salt — 28
- Trash — 30
- Happy — 31
- Unload — 32
- Transparent — 33
- God is There — 34
- Don't Give Up — 35
- Gifts — 36
- Solitaire — 37
- Overdraft Protection — 39
- Junk — 40
- Peace of Mind — 41
- Clean Up — 42
- Do you want to be Alone? — 43
- Clouds — 44
- Stand Still — 45
- Wilderness — 46
- Cracks — 47
- Harsh — 48
- Fully Charged — 49

CHAPTER 2
Spring

- Lifeline — 53
- The Right Equipment — 55
- Path — 56
- Stay Focused — 57
- Moving — 58
- Victory — 59
- Holding — 60
- Hinder — 61
- Intercede — 62
- Stand — 63
- Wake Up — 64
- Holy Spirt — 65
- Ministry — 67
- Tickets — 68
- Dry Bones — 69
- Nutrients — 70
- Who do you belong to? — 71
- Baggage — 72
- Repair — 73
- Sometimes it's not what you think — 74
- Obstacles — 76

CHAPTER 3
Summer

- Flow — 79
- Cares — 80
- Trash — 81
- Trust — 82
- Level — 83
- Sight — 84
- Crooked Places — 85
- Wash — 86
- Brokenness — 87

- Wait   89
- Right   90
- Cover   91
- Loosed   92
- Rubble   93
- Perspective   95
- Cover Up   96
- The Blood   97
- Double Check   98
- Press Through   99
- Are You Listening   100
- Patience   102
- Still Good   103

CHAPTER 4
Fall

- Merchant   107
- God's Plan   108
- Cover   109
- New   110
- New Cap   111
- Amongst The Trash   112
- Auto Save   113
- Who's Got Your Back   114
- Stand Still   115
- Clean Up   116

Foreword

When Cecelia walked into our ministry several years ago with this bright, infectious smile, I thought to myself, wonder what her story is. Well, now, I know. She is an ardent worshipper and one who demonstrates God's pure love and kindness. Her willingness to hear God and obey Him is second to none. I love the way she uses the subject "Golden Nuggets" to show how God can use our visions, dreams, and even unfavorable circumstances in our daily lives to create life-changing messages.

Reading this book reminded me of Romans 8:28 (KJV): "And we know that all things work together for good to them that love God, to them who are the called according to his purpose." Often, we are too frustrated to think about, or to look for the reasons why things happen in our lives. Cutchin reminds us that something good can come from the most devastating circumstances in life. She has compiled a litany of day to day experiences in ways that make it easy to quickly remember, that God is in total control.

Due to social, political, spiritual unrest, or personal disappointments in life, many find that there is little space in the day to recall what we already know about God. This writing reminds us that if we pay attention and learn to listen,

He will show us how to address any situation. This book is a reminder that the Lord uses our daily mishaps to teach us how to persevere in spite of them. Taking the time to seek out proper instructions and Divine directions are often our biggest hurdles. You are going to learn how to immediately delve into whatever you're going through to see what lesson should be learned.

I love the way she learned to navigate the trials and tribulations in her life and I am thankful that God impressed upon her to pen this book. In so doing, we now have a ready reference we can quickly thumb through to find encouragement, enlightenment, and empowerment to not only get us through the day but through our lives.

Overseer Dr. Priscilla H. Penn
Co-Pastor, Author, Certified Professional Life Coach
OWRAH Fellowship Ministries
Glendale, AZ

Preface

Golden Nuggets is an amazing display of the subtle lessons whispered by the voice of God. Cecelia Cutchin's brings insight to the reader understanding their struggle in today's life situations. Every Nugget presents a fresh interpretation of the Lord's deliverance and healing. She deals with practical heart felt issues that builds the reader to a place of confidence and assurance in faith and hope! Cecelia could not have picked a better time to write this book; as she opens herself to others to share some of her most deepest personal struggles that powerfully point every heart to God. Golden Nuggets challenges us to reestablish our moments of meditation to receive the written word of comfort, wisdom, and truth.

Mon'ique Simmons
Apostolic & Prophetic Network For Global Impact
Clinton, Maryland

Chapter 1
Winter

"For whoever wants to save their life will lose it, but whoever loses their life for me will find it."

Matthew 6:25

JANUARY 31, 2009

Wine

I was laying down resting. God gave me a vision of 2 wine bottles, and one was empty. The one that had wine in it, the wine was poured into the empty bottle. God said you can't mix things like that. The residue of where you came from doesn't fit to where you are going. It's like the new wine skin. Old wine can't fit in new wine skin. Matthew 2:22-And no one pours new wine into old wineskins. If he does, the wine will burst the skins, and both the wine and the wineskins will be ruined. No, he pours new wine into new wineskins." You bring the toxins, debris, and unhealthy things with you. New means adjective-of a kind now existing or appearing for the first time; adverb – recently or lately (usually used in combination). Are you trying to pour new wine into an old wine bottle or old wineskin?

FEBRUARY 26, 2009

Change

    I had come home a little after midnight from bible study on 2/25/09. My son came home from work a little behind me. I said hello and asked how he was doing. He said broke and tired. He said mom can you leave me lunch money for tomorrow. We had just prayed at bible study about giving things to God. My friend Patty had been ministering to me about I can't be the God in my children's lives. I had just laid my children and grandchild on the table at "K" and Marja's house. My response was I must pray about it. This was very difficult for me because I was used to being in mommy mode. Mommy will make it better. What you need baby? Mommy got it. No matter the cost. In 1 Peter 5:7 it says, "Cast all your cares on him, because he cares for you." Yes, my kids are spoiled, but they have lost some key people in their lives, early in their lives. My son is 22. My daughter is 19. My granddaughter is 9 months old. My dad died in March of 1996. My nephew was killed in September of 1997. My first husband, my kids' father, died in November of 1997. My baby brother died 2/2/98. My older brother died 9/30/00. Their grand- father on their father's side died 7/8/01. Their great-grand mother on their father's side died I believe in

2002. I re-married in July 1997. My husband was very strict on my kids. We got into a lot of arguments about the kids. As a result of that and his infidelity we separated in 2000. I was in a true make it better mode for my kids. It was all about them. So, when my son asked for lunch money and I said I had to pray about it, I was surprised that he did not respond "What you say mom?". However, I prayed, and God told me to give it to him in change. I was thinking it would tell my son that I didn't have much money. However, when Patty and I were riding along the next day and I shared it with her, God revealed to me that the change represented the change in my life. It represented that my son had to change his thinking. He must be more responsible with the money he gets paid to provide for himself instead of thinking "Oh I can get some money from mom". Are there areas of your life that need to be changed?

DECEMBER 3, 2009

fit

I bought some boots from Macy's online. I was excited when they arrived. I looked at the boots they were sexy. The hills weren't too high. I was anxious to wear them. I came home from work the next day and I tried the boots on. I was disappointed because I had a problem putting the boots on. I got up the sexy morning ready to try again. I figured the swelling in my feet should be down and I could put the boots on. Well, I was very disappointed when they still would not fit. You know how we are, we say "I'm going to make these fit!" God spoke to me and said that's how we do. We will try to make things fit. We know it doesn't feel comfortable. We know it is not good for our body, but we try to make it/things fit. Things that is not good for our spiritual body. Things that do not fit or agree with the Holy Spirit within us we try to make fit in our lives. When we do this, we will get scars to our body. We get calluses and pain from wearing too tight shoes. We get spiritual/mental scars from doing things that doesn't agree with the Holy Spirit within us. Matthew 6:25 says "For whoever wants to save their life will lose it, but whoever loses their life for me will find it."(NKJV) Are you trying to make things/people fit in your life? Do you have mental calluses or pain?

DECEMBER 4, 2009

Credit

I went to my attorney's office. They pulled my credit report. My credit score was low. I got depressed instantly. God spoke to me and said that is man's credit score. We need to be concerned about man's credit score, but we need to concentrate on our credit score with God. 2 Timothy 2:15 says " Study to shew thyself approved unto God, a workman that needeth not to be ashamed, rightly dividing the word of truth."(NKJV) Do you pay your bills with God on time by spending time with Him daily? Do you follow God's rules and regulations which are written in His word? What does your credit score with God look like? Does it need improving?

DECEMBER 24 2009

Lean

I was getting ready/dressed for work. I had my bible on the arm of the couch. I leaned on the bible to put my shoe on. God spoke to me and said that is what we as a people need to do. We need to lean on and trust His word. We must read it in order to lean on it. Proverbs 3:5-6 says "Trust in the LORD with all thine heart; and lean not unto thine own understanding. In all thy ways acknowledge him, and he shall direct thy paths." (NKJV) When was the last time you read your word?

DECEMBER 26, 2009

Wash

I was looking out of the window. I noticed how the rain had washed away a lot of the snow. A week prior it had snowed, and we got 22 inches of snow. God reminded me that's what he does with our sins. He washes them away. It was a WOW factor for me. Just think about it. All the sins you have done ex. fornication, lying, stealing, etc. All were washed away. God loves us that much. 1 John 1:9 says" If we confess our sins, He is faithful and righteous to forgive us our sins and to cleanse us from all unrighteousness." (NKJV) How much do you love God?

DECEMBER 31, 2009

Look

I was looking at a coat of mine debating whether to wear it. I was thinking it is New Year's Eve and I didn't want to bring the year in all tore up. My nails and eyebrows need to be done. I looked at the coat and thought about it looking nice on the outside but being all torn up on the inside. God reminded me that is how some of us are. We look good from the outside, but we are all torn up and messed up on the inside. We can wear the finest clothes, but spiritually and mentally we are all torn up. We as people especially Christians know how to put on a front. We know the Christian language. If someone asks how you are doing and you reply blessed and highly favored. We don't always have to look like what we have been through or what we're going through, but we as Christians need to let our light shine so that men can see the God in us. We as Christian people are supposed to be fishers of men. We can't draw people to us looking like a million bucks, but living our lives like we are broke, busted and disgusted. We as Christians should show some sign that our father is king of kings and lord of lords. When people listen to us and look at our lives, they should be able to tell that we are children of the most high king.

As Jill Scott says we should be living our lives like it's golden. There is another Christian song that says, "Yes they'll know we are Christians by our love".

> 1 John 4:16 says "And so we know and rely on the love God has for us. God is love. Whoever lives in love lives in God, and God in them." (NKJV)

How do you look on the inside? Can people tell you are a Christian by your love and your lifestyle?

DECEMBER 31, 2009

Tools

I was thinking that I had not used my C-Pap machine since before I went to my daughter's house on 12/13/09. A C-Pap machine helps people to breathe while sleeping because they stop breathing while sleeping (sleep apnea). Sleep apnea causes people to wake up still tired. That is because they have not had a good night's sleep. It can also cause problems with your organs because they are oxygen deprived. God reminded me that we as a people do not use some of the tools that He has given us. We don't pray. We don't read our bibles regularly. We don't surround ourselves with other believing Saints that can encourage us through hard times.

2 Timothy 3:16 says" All Scripture is breathed out by God and profitable for teaching, for reproof, for correction, and for training in righteousness." (NIV)

Are you using the tools God gave you?

JANUARY 15, 2011

Need

I was looking for some pajamas to wear to bed. I wanted to wear a certain pair, but I didn't know exactly where they were. I knew approximately where another pair of pajamas was located. As I began to look for my pajamas, I found the pair that I initially wanted to wear. God reminded me that I will supply your every need. I thought about the scripture Philippians 4:19 "And my God will supply your every need according to His riches in glory". (NKJV) I have been putting God first. I am amid a fast and consecration. Even though that may seem small to some, but I had moved my clinic to another location. I was hurting from head to toe. I was tired. I needed that clean pair of pajamas and a hot shower. I felt so much better after the shower. I got in my clean pajamas and lay in my warm bed. All of that is a blessing. I have a job. I have a home to go to. I have clothes to put on. I am blessed. All of those are needs. God cannot lie. He has supplied all my needs. AMEN!

JANUARY 16, 2011

Salt

I was reading my Women of Destiny Bible. I was reading

Matthew 5:13 "You are the salt of the earth. But if the salt loses its saltiness, how can it be made salty again? It is no longer good for anything, except to be thrown out and trampled underfoot." (NIV)

There is a letter by Betsy Neuenschwander referencing Matthew 5:13-15. It says that Jesus calls His people to be the salt of the earth. Salt (a Christian) is a preservative that retards decay it says. It states when the sprinkling of this "salt" begins, Christ's followers are observed seeking ways to preserve others. It states that in times of chaos, it is so fulfilling to be a preserver, allowing God to sprinkle us into the situation as His Holy Spirit's "sodium chloride", bringing healing and preservation. Salt is a clear brittle mineral used to flavor, preserve and deice. It is obtained by mining and evaporation; it must be crushed and ground before it can be very useful. Like salt, Christians must often be crushed before we can be of much use in God's kingdom and be a preserving force on the earth. Interestingly

the Hebrew word for salt, "malach", actually means "easily pulverized and dissolved." The Greek word for salt in Matthew 5:13 is from "halas" which figuratively means

"prudence" it states. She then asks a question. She asks, "Could it be that calamitous experiences pulverize our own foundations, fracturing our idols of self-trust, wealth, intelligence and talents?" WOW!!!! Are you salting the earth? Are you retarding/stopping decay of the souls of people? Are you allowing God to use you to bring healing and preservation? Be the salt of the earth that God has called you to be. Deice some of the hearts that have turned cold. Do you need to deice your own heart first?

JANUARY 25, 2011

Trash

I was putting my purse in my car and turned my car on to warm it up. I had reached in from the passenger side. I was going to run back into the house to get a few things while the car warmed up. As I stretched over to the driver side, I looked on the floor and saw some trash. I thought about how I was driving with that trash under my legs as if it were normal. God reminded me that is what we do as a people. We allow all different types of trash to be around us as if it is normal. God wants the best for us. We must do away with the trash in our lives even if it is in the form of people and surround ourselves with like-minded people who put God first and expect the best. We are part of a royal priesthood. 1 Peter 2:9 says" But you are a chosen people, a royal priesthood, a holy nation, God's special possession, that you may declare the praises of him who called you out of darkness into his wonderful light." (NIV) We must remember that. What trash do you have around you that you need to get rid of?

JANUARY 29, 2011

Happy

I was getting dressed for the day. I sprayed a perfume called "Happiness" on. I thought about the happiness that God pours on us. If we study the bible, the basic instruction before leaving earth, we will be happy. We know that God cannot lie, and, in the bible, it gives us instructions for being happy. If you want true happiness read and follow God's instructions. Psalm 119:130 "The unfolding of your words gives light; it imparts understanding to the simple." (ESV) When was the last time you read your instructions?

FEBRUARY 13, 2011

Unload

I had checked my glucose level. My glucometer needed some more lancets in it. As a result, I got some out of the box and put in the storage compartment in my glucometer. However, when I went to close the glucometer it was too full. I had to take some lancets out. God reminded me that we overfill our minds and lives with things. We need to unload them unto God. It says in the bible 1 Peter 5:7 "Cast all your cares on him because cares for you" (NKJV) and God will never put more on us than we can bear. 1 Corinthians 10:13 says" No temptation has overtaken you except what is common to mankind. And God is faithful; he will not let you be tempted beyond what you can bear. But when you are tempted, he will also provide a way out so that you can endure it." (NIV) We must learn to give all our cares, concerns, problems, children, family, and jobs to God. He is in control no matter how much in control we think we are. God said He would never leave us or forsake us (Heb. 13:5) and He cannot lie. Unload your cares. God cares for us.

FEBRUARY 16, 2011

Transparent

I was reading an article out of the book "Shared Blessings". It stated that when we are transparent before God and others, it keeps us clean, confessing our sin and moving us forward. It also states then we can along with the psalmist, bless the Lord with everything we have and offer our gratitude and praise without barriers or hindrance. The scripture reference is Psalm 103:1-2 "Bless the Lord, O my soul and all that is within me bless His holy name. Bless the Lord o my soul and forget not His benefits." (NKJV) It made me think, "Am I transparent to God and others? Am I transparent to myself?" We must be honest with ourselves before we can be transparent to God and others. People need us to be transparent in ministry to dispel the myth that people in ministry are perfect. God has need of people in the kingdom and He has no respect of person. He will equip you for whatever He has called you to do. However, we must be honest and transparent to ourselves first then to God and others. Are you transparent?

FEBRUARY 18, 2012

God Is There

I was looking for a pair of earrings in my jewelry drawer. I could only find one. I was about to give up looking for it. I looked down and there it was. God reminded me that sometimes we may not see it, but what we are looking for was there all the time. We may not feel God is with us sometimes, but He is there all the time. It reminds me of an old hymnal that says, "He was there all the time." Deuteronomy 31:6 says "Be strong and courageous. Do not be afraid or terrified because of them, for the LORD your God goes with you; he will never leave you nor forsake you." (NKJV) He is our keeper and sustainer. He is the lover of our soul and I thank Him.

DECEMBER 30, 2012

Don't Give Up

I was looking for a particular dress to wear for church. I had looked through several bags of clothes and was about to give up and put on a different dress. I looked in one more bag that was next to my left foot. The dress I was looking for was in that bag. God spoke and reminded me do not give up. The blessing is closer than you think. There are many times that we as people of God want to give up, but we must continue the process and get through the mess to get to our blessings. It states in Ecclesiastes 9:11 that the race is not given to the swift nor the strong but to the one that endures till the end (NKJV).

JANUARY 1, 2013

Gifts

I was lying in my bed resting and thinking. God spoke to me and reminded me that God won't spit up on you, but He will stir up the gifts in you to be used for the kingdom of God. God hath need of us. Romans 12:6-8 says "Having then gifts differing according to the grace that is given to us, let us use them: if prophecy, let us prophesy in proportion to our faith; or ministry, let us use it in our ministering; he who teaches, in teaching; he who exhorts, in exhortation; he who gives, with liberality; he who leads, with diligence; he who shows mercy, with cheerfulness." (NKJV) Our purpose is to be fishers of men. When was the last time you went fishing?

DECEMBER 18, 2014

Solitaire

I was playing Solitaire Tri-Peakes on my phone. The card came up with a bomb attached to it. If you do not get a sequential card to cut it down/the head off, it will blow up and destroy everything. The goal is to God reminded me we have the power to cut off the enemy's head. For the first time in the game, another card came up during the game with a bomb attached. God reminded me that we can yet do it again. Cut off the enemy's head. When was the last time you cut off the enemy's head?

Part 2
God said that thing/enemy will distract you. It will come after you with both barrels to put fear in you, but God. The more you rely on God the quicker the resolution to your situation.(Psalms 62:5)

Part 3
I was still playing the game. There is a button you hit to get some more cards to continue to play to try to win the game. I said I know there are no cards available, I said I am not going

to hit it because a play or two before there were none available, something (I believe it was God) said hit it anyway. I hit it and to my surprise some cards came up and I was able to win the game and God reminded me "you win". (Psalm 108:13)

Part 4
Still playing the game, a card came up with a bomb. A card did not come up from the deck to allow the head to be cut off and it blew up. God reminded me you still win because to be absent from the body is to be present with the Lord (2 Corinthians 5:8, NKJV). So even though the enemy thought he had victory, it was not so (1 Corinthians 15:55-57). God allowed it so you could be in His presence. He called you home. Your assignment was finished. Ask people who have tried to commit suicide.

Part 5
God is faithful. Every time that bomb came up except once or twice God provided a card to cut the head off. God always makes a way (1 Corinthians 10:13). It may not be the way we want or expect but it is what is best for us.

DECEMBER 31, 2014

Overdraft Protection

I was laying in the bed thinking about it being the last day of the year. I was thinking me getting my nails done and there being money in my account. They say the way you bring the year in is the way you will be during the year. I was thinking that one of my accounts was overdrawn or had a zero balance. My money market account is my overdraft protection for my checking account. God reminded me that He is our overdraft protection. Every time we are on zero or think we can't take any more, God refills us with His Holy Spirit, and we can move on in His strength. In Philippians 4:13 it says " I can do all things through Christ who strengthens me." (NKJV) We can handle whatever comes our way. Thanks be to God. Hallelujah!!!

JANUARY 9, 2015

Junk

    I was looking through my emails for my devotionals. I accidentally hit my junk tab. I saw that a God's Voice mail from the Elijah List was in that tab. The title of the devotional was "Do You Want to Learn to Hear God's Voice Better and Prophecy?" God reminded me that sometimes we discard things as junk when we should be using them/it to strengthen us. In Ecclesiastes 3:6 it says, "A time to gain, And a time to lose; A time to keep, and a time to throw away." (NKJV) What are you discarding?

JANUARY 22, 2015

Peace of Mind

While reading Pastor Rick Warren's devotional for today via email. It is entitled "The Holy Spirit". The scripture reference is John 14:27 (NLT) "I am leaving you with a gift-peace of mind." Wow!! Peace of mind is priceless. I know it for myself. Philippians 4:7 says, "And the peace of God which passeth all understanding shall keep your hearts and minds through Jesus Christ." (NKJV) People do not understand when you have peace amid chaos. The peace of God is awesome. People do not understand why you are not cussing and fussing when the job you have been on for 13 years forces you to resign. The peace of God. People cannot understand when you have been fired and they know you work hard and are normally the first one in the office and the last one to leave. The peace of God. Peace of mind is the peace of God. When you let go and let God you have peace of mind.

JANUARY 22, 2015

Clean Up

I was laying in bed thinking about how I have to go through my emails to look for some information for a meeting today. I said I need to clean up my email and delete some emails. God reminded me that that is what He does with us. He must clean us up and throw some stuff out. He must get rid of some stuff out of us. That is why we are charged to read His word and as it says we must die daily to our flesh.(1Corinth. 15:31) It is a daily clean up. When was the last time you really cleaned up?

JANUARY 23, 2015

Do you want to be Alone

I read Pastor Rick Warren's devotional for the today via email and it spoke of a counselor. It referenced John 14:16 "He will give you another Counselor." (AMP) In Ecclesiastes 3:2-8 Solomon lists twenty-eight seasons in life. As it states in the devotional, and it is true, God determines each of your life seasons. Jesus asked the Father to give us a Counselor to be with us forever. That is a long time. Jesus loved us that much. When you are not sure what to do or which way to turn seek Counsel from your personal counselor the Holy Spirit. The Holy Spirit will never steer you wrong. You're never alone unless you want to be. The song that comes to mind is "Never alone, I don't have worry cause I'm never alone." Do you want to be alone? Do you ignore your Counselor?

JANUARYY 25, 2015

Clouds

We were landing at Reagan National Airport in DC. I had just awakened from a sleep. I looked out the window. I saw white midst. I was thinking "I pray this is clouds and not snow". A very few minutes later we were through the clouds and I could see the lights on the ground. God reminded me that He clears our way through the things that cloud our lives. In Psalm 5:8 It says Lead me, O LORD, in Your righteousness because of my enemies; Make Your way straight before my face. (NKJV)

FEBRUARY 18, 2015

Stand Still

I woke up at 4:17am to use the bathroom. I went back to bed and dozed off to sleep while thinking about waking up for a 5:30am prayer call. When I woke back up it was 4:37am. God reminded me that sometimes He will allow time to stand still. It says in the word "Stand still and know that I am God" (Psalm 46:10, NKJV). He is the beginning and the end, Alpha and Omega (Revelation 1:8, NKJV). What are you worried about? What has you running to and from? Give it to God. Stand still and know that I am God. He can handle it.

DECEMBER 2, 2015

Wilderness

I was sleeping and had to go to the bathroom. I did not want to get up because I was sleeping so well. I was thinking though about being alone and on my own. It was the first night in the room that I had rented. It felt so peaceful. I did finally get up and go use the bathroom. It feels like I am in the wilderness, but I am trusting God to do just what He said. I know He can't lie. God is my source. Any job or other source of income is my resource. I WILL trust Hi. His history with me is good. God said in Hebrews 13:5 that he would never leave me nor forsake me. In this time and space, I will praise Him. I will praise my way through. And it is so.

FEBRUARY 14, 2016

Cracks

I was sitting on a couch at my girlfriend's house. I looked across the room at my purse. I began to think about how it has cracks in it. God reminded me that is how we are. We are worn, torn and tattered. I was thinking the purse does not look bad from here, but as I take a closer look, I can see the wear and tear in it. God reminded me that the closer we get to people, we can see their flaws. We can see how torn and broken they really are. In Psalms 147:3 says, "He heals the brokenhearted and binds up their wounds."

FEBRUARY 15, 2016

Harsh

I was sitting on the bed thinking about how dry my hands were. I had just finished washing dishes not long ago. I thought the water wasn't very harsh until the maintenance guy came and turned up the temperature of the water. God reminded me. That's what he has to do for us. He has to turn up the heat of life, so we don't get so comfortable. In Revelations 3:15-16 it says "I know you inside and out and find little to my liking. You're not cold, you're not hot—far better to be either cold or hot! You're stale. You're stagnant. You make me want to vomit." We need to reach our destinies. Are you in a place where you are so comfortable?

DECEMBER 4, 2019

Fully Charged

I had not long returned from a bathroom run. I began to think I needed to plug up my phone so that it could be fully charged. God reminded me that we must plug into Him so that we can be fully charged. We must be fully charged for the assignments that God has pre-destined for our lives. In 2 Timothy 2:15 it says " Study to shew thyself approved unto God, a workman that needeth not to be ashamed, rightly dividing the word of truth. In order to be fully charged we must read the Bible daily. That is our source, our fuel, our energy. Are you fully charged?

Chapter 2
Spring

"Likewise the Spirit also helps in our weaknesses. For we do not know what we should pray for as we ought, but the Spirit Himself makes intercession [a]for us with groanings which cannot be uttered."

Romans 8:26-27

APRIL 17, 2009

Lifeline

I was at lifeline. I had peeled some potatoes and was throwing the peels in the trash. I had put the peels in a plastic grocery bag while peeling the potatoes. As a I was throwing the peels in the trash, I was holding on to the bag. God spoke and asked why I was holding on to the bag. It was used. He asked why you want to hold on to something that is used when He can replace it with something new. We tend to hold on to things that are used or broken. God can give us something new for us to use. That is like the scripture about putting old things in a new wineskin. It doesn't work. The old wineskin can't hold the new wine. It will is not strong enough to hold it and has the residue of the old wine which can contaminate the new wine. (Mark 2:22-And no one puts new wine into old wineskins; or else the new wine bursts the wineskins, the wine is spilled, and the wineskins are ruined. But new wine must be put into new wineskins.) We must get past the old mind set and let God give us a new mind. Elder Zandra said that the Holy Spirit is a regeneration of the inner man or a re-gene-eration. God is giving us new genes when he fills us with the Holy Spirit. We need to allow God to re-gene us. We cannot

do it on our own in our own strength. We must let the holy spirit work in us and through us so that God can get the glory. We need to allow God free reign in the temples that he has given to us.

APRIL 18, 2009

The Right Equipment

I was washing dishes this morning. The water was starting to come out of the sink. I had the stopper in the sink which I had purchased from the dollar store. God spoke and said that the stopper was not the right type. He said that is like when we don't use the right instruments things tend to seep through. Things are not as effective. You do not get the full results because you did not use the right things. We don't want to spend the time in God's word getting to know Him better. How are we supposed to be prepared for spiritual warfare if we don't have the right equipment? We must study our bibles in order to have the right weapon for the spiritual warfare that we encounter. You can take a knife to a gun battle. We have to be soldiers for the Lord. We have to ready for the battles. We have to take the time out of our busy day to spend time with God. We have to get our instructions from our general. God is the general in charge of our lives. We have to listen to our instruction so we can have the correct shield of protection mentioned in will Psalm 91:2-I say of the LORD, "He is my refuge and my fortress, my God, in whom I trust."

APRIL 23, 2009

Path

I was driving to work on South Dakota Avenue. The left side of the street was all torn up because they were working on the road. They were also working on the right side of the street but there was smooth road and then a dip, smooth road and then a dip and so on. God spoke to me and said that's like the paths we decide to choose. If we do His will, we will have a smooth ride and then a dip every now and then, but when we choose to go our own way, we will have a rough road. We also tend to speed and go ahead of God's time. That's why we end up in a mess a lot of times. However, if we will get back on the path of God and do His will it will be a smoother ride. We will get to things in God's time and we will have a better outcome. Strive to do God's will for your life. It says in the word Joshua 24:15- And if it seems evil to you to serve the LORD, choose for yourselves this day whom you will serve, whether the gods which your fathers served that were on the other side of the River, or the gods of the Amorites, in whose land you dwell. But as for me and my house, we will serve the LORD." Will you choose to serve God or your flesh, your will, your emotions, or the devil?

MAY 20, 2009

Stay Focused

I was driving on route 495 going home. I noticed the lane to the right of me and to the left of me were full of traffic. The lane I was in was clear for about six or seven car lengths. God spoke and said "Stay Focused". He said that's like when you have things going on around you. They try to distract you, but God said stay focused. You must focus on the will of God for your life no matter what things may be going on around you. I was listening to the radio at that time and T. D. Jakes came on talking about focus. He said what you focus on is what you head toward. In Matthew 6:33 is says- But seek first the kingdom of God and His righteousness, and all these things shall be added to you. What are you focusing on? Where is your focus?

MAY 27, 2009

Moving

    I was reading Prime time with God devotional. I had my computer in my lap. My bible was on some clothes to the right of me. It was lying on my arm so I kind of pushed it to the side. God spoke to me and said that is how we do. We tend to push the word of God to the side to do what we want. Are you pushing God's word aside? It states in the Bible, Psalms 119:11-Your word I have hidden in my heart, That I might not sin against You. Do you have the word in your heart or have you pushed it aside to do your will. God gives us free will. Will you choose God or man?

MAY 28, 2009

Victory

I was walking up the escalator at work. I was singing a song by Israel and New Breed talking about victory. God reminded me that we have victory no matter how steep/hard the problems of this world may be. God has equipped us to have victory in our situations. He states in His word that He will not put any more on us than we can bear. (1 Corinthians 10:13- No temptation has overtaken you except such as is common to man; but God is faithful, who will not allow you to be tempted beyond what you are able, but with the temptation will also make the way of escape, that you may be able to bear it.) Keep that in mind the next time you are going through. Don't get stuck in the process. It is a process going thru problems, but just like when the goldsmith puts the gold in the fire. He knows it is ready when he can see himself in the gold. Can God see His reflection in you? If you quit in the process, you will be in a mess. Have faith in God. Know that he is the way maker. If you digress in the process you will not progress to success. Trust the way maker.

MAY 30, 2009

Holding

I was in the kitchen. I had used a paper plate. I threw the plate in the trash, but the new trash bag that I had put in the trash can was holding the plate up. God spoke to me and said that is like when he holds us up. We sometimes try to throw away things that we still need and may use at a later time. God will hold us up in situations and pull out of us things that we have tried to throw away. Things we did not think we needed anymore.

Psalm 18:35-36- You have also given me the shield of Your salvation; Your right hand has held me up, your gentleness has made me great. You enlarged my path under me, so my feet did not slip.

MARCH 5, 2010

Hinder

I was in the grocery store picking up a few things. I was getting something off the shelf and saw my shoe was untied. I thought to myself that I did not feel like bending over to tie the shoe. Then I thought that I needed to tie it before I trip. God spoke to me and said that is how we do. We have some things and people in our lives that can trip us up, but we don't take the time to correct or move them. We need to take the time to move things and people that will trip us up in our spiritual walk with God.

Galatians 5:7 states- You ran well. Who hindered you from obeying the truth?

MARCH 7, 2010

Intercede

I was lying in bed thinking about two of my friends. I was thinking when I noticed they were not at my son's baby shower. I was thinking that I could have picked one up. Then I remembered that there was a bad accident on the beltway where I would have had to travel. God reminded me that we sometimes avoid trouble without even knowing it. He interceded on our behalf. We don't know how many times God has done that for us. For example, God told us to go a different way and we would. Later we find out there was a major accident the way we would have gone. God instructs us to go through and we can get to our destiny. Deuteronomy 31:6 says Be strong and courageous. Do not be afraid or terrified because of them, for the LORD your God goes with you; he will never leave you nor forsake you.

MARCH 23, 2010

Stand

I was lying in bed thinking about how my weight has been going up and down since I have been trying to lose weight. God reminded me that is how life is. We go through ups and downs. God reminded me that we must stand on His word and promises. In, Ephesians, it says when you do not know what to do to stand. Ephesians 6:13-Therefore take up the whole armor of God, that you may be able to withstand in the evil day, and having done all, to stand. We must stand until God's word is clear in our lives. Once it is clear we need to move in it without hesitation. Are you standing or are you moving in your own strength?

MARCH 24, 2010

Wake Up

I was getting dressed for work. I had not turned the light on in my bedroom or straightened my bed yet. The cover was hanging partially/partly on the floor over my shoes. I stuck my foot in one shoe. It felt a little funny, but my foot was really swollen. I thought that's why it felt tight. However, when I tried to put my other foot in the other shoe I realized that it was the wrong shoe. God reminded me that is what we do. We don't pay attention to things around us and we squeeze into situations and relationships that we don't belong. We know it doesn't feel right, but we ignore it. We need to stop being sleepy Saints and wake up to what is going on around us.

Proverbs 20:13- Do not love sleep, lest you come to poverty; Open your eyes, and you will be satisfied with bread.

APRIL 21, 2010

Holy Spirit

I had taken out the trash. I came back in the house and went in my room. I felt something brush against my blanket as I was walking. I looked down and a piece of paper towel was stuck to the bottom of my right shoe. I took it off and threw it in the trash. God reminded me that is what we do. Sometimes we feel and see people are stuck to us that don't belong. We sometimes tend to ignore the signs that the Holy Spirit within us gives to us. We know the relationship or situation doesn't feel right, but we continue in it. God gives us the gift of the Holy Spirit as a protection. It is a form of alarm system. It lets you/us know when something is wrong. Would you stay in a burning building with the fire alarm going off? Even if you don't see or smell the fire, the alarm is letting you know that there is a fire or smoke somewhere. Romans 8:26-27 Likewise the Spirit also helps in our weaknesses. For we do not know what we should pray for as we ought, but the Spirit Himself makes intercession [a]for us with groanings which cannot be uttered. Now He who searches the hearts knows what the mind of the Spirit is, because He makes intercession for the saints

according to the will of God. We must listen to our alarm system the Holy Spirit. Have you listened to yours lately? Are you in a burning building?

PART TWO

I just read Lamentations 3:21-25 in my Women of Destiny Bible.

> This I recall to my mind, therefore I have hope. Through the LORD's mercies we are not consumed,
> Because His compassions fail not. They are new every morning; Great is Your faithfulness. "The LORD is my portion," says my soul, "Therefore I hope in Him! The LORD is good to those who wait for Him, To the soul who seeks Him.

There is also a letter by Doris Greig in it on that scripture. The last paragraph states that God has given us the gift of the Holy Spirit to encourage every Christian. Thus you are enabled to minister to others who are suffering because you have been there. Have you ministered to anyone lately?

APRIL 26, 2010

Tickets

God woke me up speaking in tongues. While sleeping He reminded me that we are like tickets. Some of us are speeding tickets. We speed ahead of God's plan for our lives. Some of us are like parking tickets. We need to stand still until His will is clear. However, we should not park in the wrong place. Some of us are blank tickets. We are truly waiting on the Lord. We wait to hear from the Lord to determine which way to go. Are you waiting on the Lord? Are you speeding ahead of His plan because you are tired of waiting? Psalms 27:14 says-Wait on the LORD; Be of good courage, And He shall strengthen your heart; Wait, I say, on the LORD!

MAY 3, 2010

Dry Bones

One day I was thinking about calling my ex-husband. God spoke to me and said "Why do you want to resurrect those dry bones?" I thought to myself WOW! And I did not call him. All of us have some dry bones in our lives. God reminded me of a scenario of putting water on some dry bones. Why would you want to rehydrate dry bones? They cannot do anything for you. They continue to take from you and never give back. What are you doing with the dry bones in your life? Unless you receive instructions from God like in Ezekiel 37:1-4 leave dry bones alone. Things that are dead need to be buried or cut off.

MAY 24, 2010

Nutrients

I was on my knees praying. God gave me a vision of soil being mixed up in a plant pot. It was dry, but it was dark and had silver beads in it. That usually means that it is rich in nutrients. God showed me someone pouring water on the soil. God spoke to me and said that's what the word of God(the bible) does for us. We are rich with nutrients (gifts), but the word waters us (our Spirit) so we can be the vessels God wants us to be. We can grow and become the fishers of men that God wants us to be. (Matthew 4:19-Then He said to them, "Follow Me, and I will make you fishers of men.) When was the last time you used your water (bible)?

MARCH 21, 2012

Who Do You Belong To?

I was reading 1 Samuel 17:55-58. Saul saw David going out against the Philistine (Goliath) and asked Abner the commander of his army whose son is this youth? Abner answered as your soul lives O king I do not know.

Verse 57 says "Then as David returned from the slaughter of the Philistine Abner took him and brought him before Saul with the head of the Philistine in his hand." Verse 58 "And Saul said to him "Whose son are you, young man? So David answered "I am the son of your servant Jesse the Bethlehemite."

That quickened in my spirit. "Whose daughter am I?" I am the daughter of the living God. It does not matter that I do not have a title according to man. I am who God says I am. I can do what God says I can do. I can do all things through Christ who strengthens me (Philippians 4:13). Whose son/daughter, are you?

APRIL 12, 2014

Baggage

I was looking through my bag for my homework assignment notebook for my leadership class. I found several pieces of paper that had been in my bag for weeks. They were heavy. They were making my bag heavy. They were trash. God reminded me that that is what we do. We carry around unnecessary things; this is baggage. If we would take an inventory of our lives and things we tend to worry (which is sin) about, we would be much lighter and happier if we would just "Let Go & Let God". We as people always want to "fix" things, especially us mothers. I have a saying I tell my kids when my grandchildren are crying, "Make It Better". God is the one who made it better. Jesus paid the price on Calvary. It is a done deal! Stop carrying all the unnecessary baggage. Erykah Badu has a song called "Bag Lady". I believe it says in the song at one point "Bag Lady you going to hurt your back, dragging all those bags like that." We as people hurt our backs, fronts, and even our organs (insides) worrying and carrying unnecessary stuff. Give it to God. There is a song "Jesus Paid It All, All To Him I Owe". Stop carrying things you were not meant to carry. It is a fact that stress kills. Jesus died and rose again for you and I.

****

John 8:36
Therefore if the Son makes you free, you shall be free indeed.

****

APRIL 29, 2014

Repair

I was thinking about my new house. I was thinking that it is a little messed up and tore down now but when the remodeling/repairs are done it will look brand new. God reminded me that is how we are. We are tore down and in need of repair until He fixes us up. He fills us with His Holy Spirit and makes us brand new. Thank you, God.

2 Corinthians 5:17-Therefore, if anyone is in Christ, he is a new creation; old things have passed away; behold, all things have become new.

MAY 15, 2015

Sometimes It's Not What You Think

    I was putting my jewelry on for the day. I had laid out my silver link chain necklace and earring set, or so I thought. I put on one earring. As I went to put on the other earring, I realized that the hook to the other earring was missing. I began to look through the bag that my jewelry was stored in. I was thinking I saw a hook without an earring and was wondering what earring it belonged to not long ago. Now I see an earring without a hook and wonder where the hook is. I even examined the earring to see how the hook could have come off and saw a place in the hoop of one of the links of the chain where it was separated. I started to push it back together but thought I may need to put the hook in this spot first. I began to look through the bag and found another link chain earring. I thought "What?" Did I buy a second pair of link chain earrings at some point? However, as I began to observe more closely, what I realized and remembered was that my necklace had broken previously, and I put the broken links in the bag with my jewelry. That was an "Aha" moment. What I originally thought was my other earring was actually my

broken link from my necklace. Sometimes things are not what you think they are. God reminded me things are not going the way I thought they would during my transition. I thought to myself God really got jokes. God does not always do things the way you expect, but it's for your good. To God be the glory.

Isaiah 55:8-For My thoughts are not your thoughts, nor are your ways My ways," says the LORD.

MARCH 7, 2016

Obstacles

    I was walking in my room. I began to step over some things on the floor. I was thinking, "Don't step over them, move them out od the way." God began to speak as I began to throw things away from off the floor. These were things that I didn't need that were in my way. He said that he is going to start removing things spiritually out of my life that is hindering my walk with him, just like those things were hindering my physical walk in the room. I was supposed to be on a prayer call but when God speaks to you directly you must take time to listen.

Chapter 3
Summer

" Be anxious for nothing, but in everything by prayer and supplication, with thanksgiving, let your requests be made known to God; and the peace of God, which surpasses all understanding, will guard your hearts and minds through Christ Jesus."

Philippians 4:6-7

JUNE 1, 2009

Flow

My friend Patty and I were on our way home from class. There was a backup of traffic on the beltway. I saw a big yellow arrow letting me know that a lane was closed. I rode in the far-right lane until it merged onto a ramp. I then got back over into the traffic lanes and the lanes were clear. I passed all that traffic. Patty said you were able to get to the other side and I added, and things were clear. She said now you can flow. It stuck in my spirit and I was ready to get out and shout on the beltway. God will allow you to pass a lot of junk/mess so that when you get to the other side you can flow. You can flow in the things of God without hindrances. Romans 12:1-2"So here's what I want you to do, God helping you: Take your everyday, ordinary life—your sleeping, eating, going-to-work, and walking-around life—and place it before God as an offering. Embracing what God does for you is the best thing you can do for him. Don't become so well-adjusted to your culture that you fit into it without even thinking. Instead, fix your attention on God. You'll be changed from the inside out. Readily recognize what he wants from you, and quickly respond to it. Unlike the culture around you, always dragging you down to its level of immaturity, God brings the best out of you, develops well-formed maturity in you."{MSG} How is your flow?

JUNE 2, 2009

Cares

I was in the shower. The water was coming down on my shoulders. It felt so good. It was taking away the pain. God spoke and said that is like the Holy Spirit falling down on you. It removes the burdens off your shoulders. You feel much lighter. Sometimes you don't realize how heavy your burdens are to bear. It says in the Bible 1 Peter 5:7 to cast your cares on God for He cares for you. A lot of time we try to take care of things ourselves on our own strength. Especially us women, we have that fix it mentality. We have got to make it better because we are mommy. That is why it is so hard for us to turn our children over to God. We sometimes become the God in our children's lives and we don't even realize it. They have the mentality; no matter the age, that mommy can fix it. Mommy will take care of it and a lot of times we do. However, we must let God deal with our children. It is not easy, but it is necessary. Are you trying to carry your burdens, problems, children?

JUNE 3, 2009

Trash

I was cleaning my room. I saw a piece of paper from my pantyhose on the floor. God said "Throw it away." I said "I am God". He said "Now!" I picked it up and threw it away. We tend to want to hold on to things ex. Trash, unhealthy relationships, situations, and people when God tells us to throw away or do away with something or someone. We need to do it immediately or as Elder Peyton said, we will deal with the debris or residue of that thing. In 2 Corinthians 5:17-20 (MSG)- Now we look inside, and what we see is that anyone united with the Messiah gets a fresh start, is created new. The old life is gone; a new life burgeons! Look at it! All this comes from the God who settled the relationship between us and him, and then called us to settle our relationships with each other. God put the world square with himself through the Messiah, giving the world a fresh start by offering forgiveness of sins. God has given us the task of telling everyone what he is doing. We're Christ's representatives. God uses us to persuade men and women to drop their differences and enter God's work of making things right between them. We're speaking for Christ himself now: Become friends with God; he's already a friend with you.

AUGUST 3, 2009

Trust

I came in my office and started putting my laptop docking station back together. However, in doing so I realized that I did not have to take it apart to take the laptop out. I thought too much about the process. All I had to do was push a button to lift the laptop from the docking station. However, I went to the back of the station and unhooked wires. That was only necessary when putting the station together. God said to me that is what we do. We over think situations. We stress and fear instead of relaxing, relating and resting. If we relax we can think more clearly. If we relate the process to something familiar, we can come up with a better solution. Moreover, if we rest the situation or problem in God's hands we do not have to worry, fear or fret. God has it all in control. In Proverbs 3:5-6- Trust in the LORD with all your heart and lean not on your own understanding; In all your ways acknowledge Him, and He shall direct your paths.

JUNE 4, 2010

I was sitting in the home going service for Pastor Geraldine McInnis. I had to go up to sing with the choir. I was thinking about how lose my shoes were on my feet. I thought to myself that these shoes used to fit. God spoke to me and said that things that used to fit don't fit anymore. God said He is taking me to a different level. I thank God for the elevation. Are you going to a new level in God or are you staying stagnant and stuck? 1 John 2:27- But the anointing that you received from him abides in you, and you have no need that anyone should teach you. But as his anointing teaches you about everything, and is true, and is no lie—just as it has taught you, abide in him.

APRIL 21, 2010

Sight

    I came back to work after being out on sick leave for one and a half weeks. My desk looked filthy. The first thing I did was clean my desk. I thought to myself it didn't look that bad when I left. God spoke to me and said that is like when we do not see things for what they really are because we have gotten used to it. We need to step back from certain situations and go back at another time to take a look at it and evaluate. It says in 2 Corinthians 4:18 - while we do not look at the things which are seen, but at the things which are not seen. For the things which are seen are temporary, but the things which are not seen are eternal. Are you doing what God would have you to do? Are you where God wants you to be? Don't get so caught up in everyday life doing the same old thing that you can't see the forest for the trees.

JULY 11, 2010

Crooked Places

    I was unbending a hanger in which to hang my clothes. Jesus reminded me that he would make the crooked places straight. (Isaiah 45:2) What crooked places do you have in your life? You need to turn them over to God. Evaluate your life. Make sure everything you say and do give God glory. Are you giving God glory?

JULY 14, 2010

Wash

    I was washing dishes. There was a plastic Ziploc bowl that I picked up. I thought about throwing it out because it was so greasy. I decided to try to wash it to see how it turned out. I washed it and it was practically good as new. God reminded me that is how we are. We are covered with a lot of stuff/junk. We get into God's word and doing His will and all of that stuff is washed off. However, we have to submit to His will. What do you look like? Are you carrying a lot of stuff/junk? Give it to God. Submit to his will. Ephesians 4:22-24 "You were taught, with regard to your former way of life, to put off your old self, which is being corrupted by its deceitful desires; to be made new in the attitude of your minds; 24 and to put on the new self, created to be like God in true righteousness and holiness."

JULY 15, 2010

Brokenness

I was reading my Women of Destiny Bible. I was reading the letter to coincide with 2 Chronicles 6:30 about need. The letter starts off by talking about brokenness. It talks about the release of the Holy Spirit through brokenness. It states brokenness is walking in the bright light of the truth about myself as I am before God, and immediately He reveals to me a sin, which inevitably causes darkness. It also states that through confession, repentance and restitution, I walk on in full light again. It references Isaiah 2:5 "Come and let us walk in the light of the Lord." Further in the letter it talks about when the woman broke the alabaster flask of very costly oil and poured it over Jesus' head as an act of devotion to him. It states by doing that she broke through the barrier of fear of men. It references that Jesus then broke through with His unique acclamation of approval of her insight and devotion, even saying that she would be remembered wherever the gospel would be proclaimed. The fragrance of that oil would linger on Jesus and be sensed by everyone who came in contact with Him and the scripture reference is Mark 14:3-9. It reminded me that we need to remain in some form of brokenness so the

Holy Spirit can constantly use us. It also made me think about hoe Jesus smelled. I can imagine a sweet smell of frankincense and Mur. I also thought about how we may smell to Jesus. Do you smell rotten? Are you

a sweet smell in the nostrils of our Lord? Remain in a state of brokenness.

JULY 19, 2010

Wait

I was driving to work. I would normally take Tuxedo Road to the parking lot on South Dakota Avenue. If the curve of Tuxedo Road is crowded or slow, I go to the second curve. Traffic was a little slow so I went to the second curve. I always look where I would be had I took the first curve by looking at the car I would have been behind. I would check to see if I beat it by going to the second curve. This morning I didn't beat the car would have been behind. As a matter of fact, I was two cars behind where I would have been. God reminded me that we sometimes think we are getting ahead but we need to be patient and wait on God. His timing is perfect. It says in Psalms 27:14 "Wait on the Lord, be of good courage and He shall strengthen thy heart. Wait I say on the Lord. "It realizes we can be a little hard head so it tells us twice to wait on the Lord. Are you trying to run ahead of God? Be patient and wait.

JULY 24, 2010

Right

I was straightening up my bed. The tag on the comforter that is normally at the bottom of the bed was at the top. God spoke to me and said some things that look wrong to other or backwards to others are right or the right way in His sight. Even though something may look or be wrong by man's standards, as long as it's right by God's standard that's all that matters. In Deuteronomy 6:18-19 it says "And you shall do what is right and good in the sight of the LORD, that it may be well with you, and that you may go in and possess the good land of which the LORD swore to your fathers, to cast out all your enemies from before you, as the LORD has spoken."

JULY 26, 2010

Cover

Part 1

I had fallen asleep watching TV in the basement. I woke up and got up at 2:22 am. I was lying in my bed and I thought about my bible it was lying on an exotic toy brochure on the table in the basement. My friend's daughter had started selling Tupperware and exotic toys. She had a combination party. I thought about how the bible was covering the toy catalogue on the table. God reminded me that's what he does for us. His love covers a multitude of sins. Jesus died on the cross for our sins. What a love. How much do you love God? Do you study His word? Do you have a good relationship with Him? Examine yourself. What do you need to do differently to improve your love for God?

In *1 Peter 4:8- And above all things have fervent love for one another, for "love will cover a multitude of sins."*

Loosed

Part 2

    I was reading my bible. I read Acts 16:25-26. It tells about how Paul and Silas were in prison yet they were praying and singing hymns to God. It says he other prisoners were listening to them. It says suddenly there was a great earthquake so that the foundations of the prison were shaken and immediately all the doors were opened and everyone's chains were loosed. God reminded me that because I praise Him, my chains will be loosed. My emotional, my physical and all other types of chains will be loosed but, I must praise Him in every situation. What type of prison are you in? Are you in chains? Praise your way loose.

AUGUST 16, 2010

Rubble

I was reading the book "From The Father's Heart" given to me by my Godmother. It is a book of letters from God given to author Charles Slagle. I was reading on entitled "Removing the Rubble". It references Nehemiah 4:2; I Corinthians 3:11-16 and Hebrew 6:1-3. It states at present I am rebuilding your walls, but there is rubble which first must be swept away. Now I am showing you what the rubble is, why it came to be, and how it is to be removed. So be patient with yourself, and be patient with me. It states some of the rubble is bits and pieces of an earlier "you" which was truly good, but was destroyed when the enemy took advantage of your youth. That was a real WOW moment for me. I thought back to some of the things that I did in my youth and I am thankful to God that He kept me. I am thinking is there any rubble in my life today/now that I need to pray to God to remove. It also states that there are some odd shaped fragments. It says those are scraps from the materials you used when you once set out to rebuild your own walls. Thankfully, the plan was aborted before it really began to take shape. That will mean less work and time saved for both you and God provided you, resist the urge to analyze

every piece and get on with the job of clearing them out. I thought back to how many times I tried to do things on my own and analyze it when it went wrong in my eyes. God is just awesome. Allow God to remove the rubble and rebuild the walls in your life.

AUGUST 17, 2010

Perspective

I went to the post office. On the way out I looked at the exit doors. I wondered which door was open. One of them had a latch to push and open the door. I knew that if you pushed it the door would open. The other door didn't have a latch and I figured it would be easier to open. As a result, I pushed the door with no latch. It was locked. So I had to push the door with the latch to get out. God reminded me that is how we do. We choose the way that looks the easiest. However, we know if we really trust and wait on God it is a guarantee. We need to be patient and wait on God's leading in every situation for we know even though it may look hard, but it is the guaranteed right way to go. What looks good or easy to you is not always good for you. Wait and trust in God.

In Proverbs 14:12 it says, "There is a way that seems right to a man, but its end is the way of death."

AUGUST 19, 2010

Cover Up

I was thinking about a photo album in which the back cover came off. I was thinking that I needed some white electronic tape to put it back together so it won't look so bad because the photo album is white. God reminded me that we tend to cover things up so they/we don't look bad. What are you trying to cover up? If we turn things (people, situations) over to God we won't have to try to cover them up. Maybe God is even using you to show somebody how a situation should be handled. Don't cover up, give it up. Give everything to God He is the burden bearer. In Isaiah 53:4-5 it says "Surely, he took up our pain and bore our suffering, yet we considered him punished by God, stricken by him, and afflicted. But he was pierced for our transgressions, he was crushed for our iniquities; the punishment that brought us peace was on him, and by his wounds we are healed."

AUGUST 23, 2010

The Blood

On 8/20/10 some friends and I were getting prepared to leave on vacation to Myrtle Beach, S.C. We were planning to leave on 8/21/10. My friend from New Jersey was talking to me and another friend about her sister who had gotten hit upside her head with a bowl by her husband. The bowl was glass. He threw it hat her. She called the police, but when they got there, she decided not to file charges. She was also five months pregnant. There would have been nothing they could do if they had not seen some blood sliding down her neck. Her hair was long, but the blood came streaming down. That reminded me how Jesus died on the cross for us. They pierced him in his hands and put a thorn bush on his head. The blood was streaming down. He died for our sins. If they (the enemy) had not seen the blood of Jesus can you imagine where we would be? Thank you Jesus for your blood and for your sacrifice. We owe him a sacrifice of praise and thanksgiving. When was the last time you made that sacrifice? In John 19 it tells of the crucifixion of Christ.

JUNE 10, 2013

Double Check

I went to a revival service with one of my friends. The Pastor preached "My Nightmare Is Over". He referenced 2 John 7-12. It talks about men who had leprosy. It talks about how they say if they don't go into the camp that they would die. They were hungry and needed food. However, because they were "unclean" they were not supposed to go into the camp. The people may kill them for coming in. So, if they stayed out, they would die for sure but, if they went in, they might die. So, they trusted God and went in the camp.

As I was trying to read along with the scripture, my version was a very different version from what the preacher was reading. I confirmed the scripture with my friend. On my tablet it looked to be in the right spot. However, when I reset the coordinates on the tablet it went to the correct verses of scripture. Sometimes we must double check to make sure we are in the right position with God. We must trust that God will make a way. Are you in the right position? Has God made a way for you?

JUNE 17, 2013

Press Through

    I was going to meet with Apostle Karen Spriggs. When I got to the Oxon Hill area, I ran into a rainstorm. I could barely see in front of me. I though about turning around and going home. However, I decided to press on. I drove through the storm in a few minutes. Later, as I crossed the Woodrow Wilson Bridge I ran into another storm. I was praying and said, "God really?" However, I drove through that storm in a few minutes. When I arrived at Apostle's home, we had a glorious time in God. God had me to realize that we must press through storms of life. There is sunshine and victory on the other side of the storm. We must trust that God will bring us through. Philippians 3:14 says " I press toward the goal for the prize of the upward call of God in Christ Jesus." Do you trust God? Are you resting and relying on him?

JUNE 21, 2013

Are You Listening

I was in the bathroom. I remembered about taking medication per my doctor's instructions to help my ear. My ear started bothering me about two weeks prior. It stopped up and felt like I was in a plane or a tunnel. I went on for a few days periodically. It then became a consistent feeling in my ear. I put peroxide in it to clean it out. I went to the doctor after seven days of irritability for evaluation. She said it looked fine, but she couldn't see the ear drum of the one that I could hear out of because of the wax build up.

She had me to use Debrox in that ear over the weekend and come back Monday of the following week for follow up. I followed up per her instructions and I still could not hear out of the ear. As a result, she referred me to an ENT (ear, nose and throat) physician. As I was in the bathroom, I though about how irritating it was not to be able to hear out of that ear.

God reminded me if you don't want to listen to me, I can take away your hearing. It was a "Wow!" moment for me. I also thought about how irritating it is for me not to be able to hear.

JULY 23, 2016

Still Good

I was looking for a colored marker to do some mind mapping. I remembered that I had some in my bag with my prayer sheet. First, I pulled the new bag I had purchased to carry the prayer sheet. I thought, "Oh yes! I need to change bags." Then, I began to look for the different colors that I had available. I began to take the sheets and the markers out of the old bag. I was thinking" Yes, this has a whole in it. I need to throw it away."

As I evaluated, the bag, I discovered the whole was located where the handle of the bag was extending from the bag. It only had a little tear. I thought. "his bag is still good." God reminded me that even though people may think we are trash or no good, we are "still good to Him. When we are in the hands of our father (reading the bible, worship, praying) on a regular basis, He can mold us and make us to be used for His good.

In Isaiah 64:8 it says "But now, O LORD, you are our Father; we are the clay, and you our potter; and all we are the work of your hand. (NKJV) God is a gentleman. He doesn't force us. We must submit to his will. My prayer is "His will and his way." To God be all the glory. Amen. WE ARE STILL GOOD!

I thought how irritating it must be for God when we don't listen and follow his word.

The Bible is the basic instruction before leaving the earth. Isaiah 28:23 says, "Give ear and hear my voice, listen and hear my speech." Are you listening to God and following his instructions?

PART 2

I was reading my "Bible Promises Book for Women". It was discussing pride. It referenced Proverbs 1:33 which says "But whoever listens to me will dwell safely, and will be secure, without fear of evil." I want to be secure and safe without ear of evil in God. So, I must listen. Do you want to be safe and secure?

JULY 1, 2014

Patience

    I was driving to work on a busy, main street. I pulled up behind an 18-wheeler truck. We were at a red light. When the light changed, the truck moved very slowly. I waited for the traffic in the left lane to clear and I moved to the left lane and passed the truck. I didn't think the truck would move so slowly. God reminded me that that's how we are. We think things are going to move at a fast pace. When it moves slowly, we think we should have known. Things don't always go as planned or anticipated. However, we must remember God is in control and His time is not our time. In Philippians 4:6-7 says " Be anxious for nothing, but in everything by prayer and supplication, with thanksgiving, let your requests be made known to God; and the peace of God, which surpasses all understanding, will guard your hearts and minds through Christ Jesus." But as Pastor Peyton said on Sunday, we all have an issue with patience. What comes to mind is the Serenity Prayer: God grant me the serenity to accept the things I cannot change, the courage to change the things I can and the wisdom to know the difference.

Chapter 4
Fall

"Nor do they put new wine into old wineskins, or else the wineskins break, the wine is spilled, and the wineskins are ruined. But they put new wine into new wineskins, and both are preserved."

Matthew 9:17

November 3, 2013

Merchant

I was lying down trying to get back to sleep. I had awakened to go to the bathroom. I heard "He is a merchant of "good" care not "you" care". God gives you what is good for you, not necessarily what you want. In His word He states He will supply your every need according to His riches in glory (Philippians 4:19). Your need may not be what you want. God knows what is best for you. The definition of merchant is a person or company involved in wholesale trade especially one dealing with foreign countries or supplying merchandise to a particular trade, per Google dictionary. WOW! God deals with trading. He will trade our bad for good. He uses our troubles to strengthen us. He deals with foreign countries and foreign spirits. He has equipped us with the merchandise/equipment to deal with spirits in the form of the Holy Spirit. The Holy Spirit lets us/you know what is good for us/you. We do not always listen. Keep in your mind this question, "Will what you do to give God glory?". We are Ambassadors for Him. Give Him glory.

OCTOBER 26, 2015

God's Plan

I was traveling on route 270 driving Uber. I started to change lanes. I saw an opening in the lane to the left of me. I decided to stay in the lane in which I was currently driving. The car in front of me moved into that open spot. I thought to myself " I should've taken advantage of that opportunity when I had the chance." However, suddenly the lane that I was traveling in began to move and I passed the car that was in front of me previously. God reminded me that sometimes when you think you have missed me, you are just where I want you to be and I will expedite the process for you. Continue to seek God's face and he will do the rest. In Philippians 4:19 is says " And my God shall supply all your need according to His riches in glory by Christ Jesus." He is not a man that he should lie. (Numbers 23:19)

NOVEMBER 8, 2015

Cover

I was getting dressed. I had put on a pair of designer pantyhose. They were black and grey. They have zigzag lines that looked like rays of thunder on them. As I put them on I saw there was a small whole on the leg. I was thinking that I could not wear them because I am on the praise and worship team. People will see it when I am up front singing. I was running late for church. I did not have time to change them. I grabbed a pair of regular black pantyhose. I said that I would change at church after praise team rehearsal. When I put my dress on, it was so long you could not see the whole in my pantyhose. God reminded me. That is the way God does things for us. He covers our sins. What looks large to us is small to Him. I thank God for covering me. God gives beauty for ashes as it states in Isaiah 61:3.

NOVEMBER 9, 2015

New

I was getting dressed. I was looking for a pair of pantyhose to wear that I had already worn. I knew that I had several pair that I had the day before. God spoke to me and said, "Why are you looking for something old when I want to give you something new?" I had some new pantyhose in a bag on the other side of the bed. I had to chuckle to myself and say, "Ok God." Philippians 3:13-14 says it like this " Brethren, I do not count myself to have [d]apprehended; but one thing I do, forgetting those things which are behind and reaching forward to those things which are ahead, I press toward the goal for the prize of the upward call of God in Christ Jesus."

DECEMBER 19, 2016

Auto Save

I had been working on a homework assignment from late evening until early morning. I decided to lay down and get a few hours of sleep and get back up to complete the assignment. When I got back up and started searching for the assignment, I realized I had forgotten to save the assignment. However, over in the left corner of the Windows screen there was as pop-up of several documents that had auto saved.

The document that I needed had auto saved. You can imagine my joy that I did not have to start all over again. I had not lost all that work! God spoke to me and said, "Auto saved." Jesus auto saved us when he died on the cross for our sins. He hung there and died. We do not have to worry but we must confess our sins. Auto saved!

It says in John 3:16 "For God so loved the world that He gave His only begotten Son, that whoever believes in Him should not perish but have everlasting life." (NKJV)

When was the last time you auto saved someone for the sins, they have done against you? Press "auto save" says the Lord.

DECEMBER 20, 2016

Who's Got Your Back

I was up doing my hair thinking about my son and his position in life at the present time. I was praying for God to turn things around for him. I thought about a situation concerning his license and an accident he was involved with on his job. I thought the circumstances would have been better if his job had backed him like they said they would. But I thought, that's okay because God has his back. God reminded me that he would never leave you nor forsake you. In Hebrews 13:5-6 it says "5 Let your conduct be without covetousness; be content with such things as you have. For He Himself has said, "I will never leave you nor forsake you." So, we may boldly say The LORD is my helper; I will not fear. What can man do to me?" God always has your back, your front, and your sides. Who has got your back? Who are you serving? Do you spend time with God? He's got my back.

NOVEMBER 17, 2015

New Cap

I had awakened from falling asleep with my clothes still on. I went to the bathroom. I was trying to get oriented and move things off my bed. I noticed a new shower cap that I had purchased over the weekend in a bag. I thought to myself that I could have used it the day before when I took a shower. I thought about the situation and realized my old cap is just fine. God spoke to me and said, "Why do you insist on using the old, when I'm trying to give you new?" Matthew 9:17 says "Nor do they put new wine into old wineskins, or else the wineskins break, the wine is spilled, and the wineskins are ruined. But they put new wine into new wineskins, and both are preserved."

God spoke to me and said "Daughter that's why I am moving you. Where I am taking you, there will be new friends. The atmosphere you are in will not be ale to hold where I am taking you. Trust me." I said, "Yes Lord."

OCTOBER 27, 2016

Amongst The Trash

I was cleaning my room. I was sweeping the floor. I heard God say, "Amongst the trash." I looked down at what had been swept in the trash. There were some bobby pins. I needed them for my hair. There was a business card of someone I had met at one of my business conferences. There was another business card of two men I had met at a business conference in Atlanta. Their company name is "Vision". God reminded me that we should be careful what we put amongst the trash. There was also money, amongst the trash. We should be careful not to throw out things that should be kept. However, those things, relationships that God has told us to do away with we must put away. It could not only cause detriment to our physical beings but also spiritual beings. In 1 Corinthians 6:19-20 it says " Or do you not know that your body is the temple of the Holy Spirit who is in you, whom you have from God, and you are not your own? For you were bought at a price; therefore glorify God in your body [g]and in your spirit, which are God's." (NKJV) Always evaluate what you put amongst the trash.

FEBRUARY 5, 2018

Stand Still

I woke up at 4:17 am to use the bathroom. I went back to bed and fell asleep. I did not want to miss the 5:30 am prayer call. I woke back up to verify the time. It was only 4:37 am. God reminded me that sometimes he will allow time to stand still. In Psalms 46:10 it says "Be still, and know that I am God." He is the beginning and the end, Alpha and Omega. What are you worried about? What has you running back and forth? Give it to God. Stand still and know that I am God. He can handle it.

NOVEMBER 28, 2019

I was washing dishes. I used the power hose to clean the sink. There is one located beside the faucet. God reminded me to use the tools he gave me to clean/clear away the clutter. He reminded me that I have power, to use it. In Luke 10:19 it says "Behold, I give you the authority to trample on serpents and scorpions, and over all the power of the enemy, and nothing shall by any means hurt you."

About the Author

Cecelia is an experienced worshipper in an evolving relationship with God and the ministering of His divine Word. Driven by this love, she has taken joy in providing the best ministry and guidance possible through lived life experiences. Cecelia's passion for God can be traced back to childhood where she spent significant time singing and praising God. This relationship encouraged her to treat people the way God and she would like to be treated.

As a Center Manager her goals include treating people the way that she wants to be treated and providing excellent customer service. In addition to her primary job functions, Cecelia has been recognized by several ministries for her extraordinary commitment to excellence. As a minister and writer, she specializes in delivering God's messages in love.

Notes

CPSIA information can be obtained
at www.ICGtesting.com
Printed in the USA
BVHW062031020321
601494BV00010B/845